LEANING IN
30 DAY REMNANT DEVOTIONAL
preparing for encounter

Copyright © 2023 by Amanda Crabb

All rights reserved. No portion of this book may be reproduced in any form without written permission from the publisher or Amanda Crabb, except as permitted by U.S. copyright law.

This book is dedicated to my husband, Aaron, and our beautiful children. You truly are Levitical in nature. I am proud of your passionate pursuit of encounter and your heart that desires to create a space for others to have this same experience.

While I may hold many roles and titles, being called wife and mom is my favorite of them all! I love you!

ACKNOWLEDGEMENTS

There are so many in my life who make what I do possible. I am very aware that without them, there would be no Restoring Hope Church or Amanda Crabb Ministries.

First and foremost, our staff at RHC, you are phenomenal! Thank you for your constant leaning in at our table. You carry a weight alongside of us that cannot be expressed in words or denied by deed. Your purity and passion are what make RHC so special. Thank you for your diligence in the work and your dedication to keep the anointing pure. You are those who will pick up all the scattered pieces of creativity and make a beautiful picture come forth. We are aware that each of you could sit at any table, and we don't take it for granted that you choose to sit with us. You never ask what we are serving, but you still always come hungry. We love you!

Ty Hicks, our media manager. There isn't enough room on these pages to define what you do. Thank you for hearing the voice of God at Overflow 2021! Your obedience to say what you saw opened up a whole new world to me. You were an answer to a prayer prayed. You knew how to do what I didn't, and here we are, two years in and releasing Volume 1 of Remnant Devotions. It's amazing how Kingdom, remnant pieces work together, and I am so blessed to have you as a piece in our puzzle. Thank you for helping me minister to these amazing people.

The body of Restoring Hope church and Remnant Mentees, thank you for allowing me to be a voice in your life. You are a people who are truly defined as "believers." Your faith and trust aren't in human ability, but it is the one true God through the power of Jesus' name. In a world filled with so much noise, you are the people who desire to lean in and hear a directive from the Holy Spirit because you know that His voice will lead you to truth, and His truth opens the door to encounter!

Finally, I would like to express my gratitude to all the teachers who have impacted my life: Ronna Harrison, Darlene Bishop, Sandy Farhart, John and Diana Hagee, Todd Hoskins, Jack Midkiff, Pastor Rod Parsley, and all the professors at Valor Christian College. I have learned so much from each of your lives. You've set the example to remain humble and teachable and showed me how to love God and His people. These are just a few of my favorite attributes that each of you possess and that I aspire to. Thank you for leading the way so others can have an encounter. You are all part of my story, and I am grateful for that.

TABLE OF CONTENTS

1	IF NOT YOU, THEN WHO?	17
2	THE ALTAR IN YOUR HOME	19
3	CHANGE YOUR POSITION	21
4	CREATE A SPACE	23
5	PARTIAL OBEDIENCE	25
6	DON'T STOP SHORT	27
7	STAY FOCUSED	29
8	IN SPIRIT AND IN TRUTH	33
9	ESCAPE VS ENCOUNTER	35
10	OBEDIENCE OR SACRIFICE	37
11	THROUGH OR TO	39
12	POSTURE OVER POSITION	41
13	LIVE IN ENCOUNTER	43
14	DON'T GET DISTRACTED	45
15	DECLARE THE WORD	49
16	MORE THAN A CONQUEROR	51
17	KEEP DECLARING	53
18	CONSISTENCY IS KEY	55
19	YOU'VE BEEN TESTED	57
20	ALL THINGS ARE POSSIBLE	59

TABLE OF CONTENTS

21	DREAM AGAIN	61
22	THE RAIN IS HERE	65
23	HARVEST IS YIELDING	67
24	DRY AND BARREN SEASON	69
25	NO TANGIBLE EVIDENCE	71
26	TEND THE RIGHT THINGS	73
27	LOOK ONE MORE TIME	75
28	HURRY, THE RAIN WILL STOP YOU	77
29	BE A FRIEND	81
30	MOVE FORWARD	83

FOREWARD

I remember several years ago, a man at a Regis hair salon began speaking over my wife. She had been praying and asking God what He would want to do through her life, and with tears streaming down her face, she received the words of this prophecy concerning her; "You carry a teaching anointing, and you are chosen for such a time as this." This prophecy was given in a season when she couldn't even picture what a teaching anointing would look like, but she received it in full confidence that if Jesus said it, it would come to pass.

I've witnessed the first of many things in her life. I was there the day she was filled with the power of God. The day she became a mom for the first time. I've watched her tell her testimony in a room full of a thousand people and heard her preach countless public sermons over the last 18 years, but most importantly, I've witnessed her private devotion to Jesus. Her words spoken in our home and behind a pulpit have empowered and encouraged me through the years. To keep going, never give up, and always to stay hungry for more.

Jesus was often found reclining at tables with His disciples. A place of natural hunger became a place to birth spiritual hunger. I know and understand Amanda's heart better than anyone on this earth and

FOREWARD

I know her heart for you is that you would relax, find peace in Jesus, and gather your family at a table to communicate what He is speaking to you through these devotionals. Give a place for your family to discuss biblical things in a manner that isn't "religious" but "relational." Amanda has a God-given gift to tie everyday life to biblical truth. It is this very gift that has cultivated our home to be a place of presence and peace.

So I now encourage you to lean in because I believe this 30-day devotional will be a tool for the journey and a key to unlocking promise in your life and in your family!

Aaron Crabb
Lead Pastor of Restoring Hope Church
Author of **Next**

HEY, REMNANT!

Today, you're consciously deciding to move into the very promise God spoke over your life. You can feel a pull that you cannot explain, but you know it's from God. You're part of the Remnant, the remaining few with a distinct purpose in this day and time.

Regardless of your age, race, and upbringing, you know God is calling you higher than the place you are familiar with, the groups you have been entertaining, and the rooms you have been standing in. Recognizing this isn't a bad thing; it's needed to take a step. As the scripture says, "Trust in the Lord with all your heart..." because once the journey starts, you can't look to man to do what only God can.

Lean In, receive instruction, and prepare for the encounter that will lead you to your next!

—Amanda Crabb

en·coun·ter

en'koun(t)ər/

---

*an unexpected face to face experience
[that changes everything]*

Week One

DAY 1
IF NOT YOU, THEN WHO?

I believe we are entering a season where God gives insight and instruction to His people willing to carry out the Word. We have lived in a day where people have had great, Godly ideas but no action behind God's speaking. God is giving insight and wisdom on what to do with the ideas He has given. Noah had never seen rain when he was chosen to build the Ark, but He trusted God so much that he began to build. Noah did not have the wisdom to build such a great boat, but God did. God spoke wisdom, and Noah carried out the Word. God is looking for people to carry out the Word He has been saying.

We have gotten too comfortable with someone else carrying the Word, but God is looking for a Remnant to pick up the pieces others have dropped and create something extraordinary. I wonder how many ideas are lying in graveyards across the world. I said it a few weeks ago from the pulpit; if not you, then who? If not now, then when? We have allowed too many Words from the Lord to fall to the ground. It's time to pick up the Word and run with it!

> *"For the Lord gives wisdom; From His mouth come knowledge and understanding"*
> **-Proverbs 2:6**

Journal

What insight has God given you?
What has He asked you to do this season?
Have you started? If not, what do you need to
take to get going? Write them down.

_____
_____
_____
_____
_____
_____
_____
_____
_____
_____
_____
_____
_____

DAY 2
THE ALTAR IN YOUR HOME

The Church is made up of individual homes. If the church is weak, it's because our body's houses are weak. Moving into this season, I don't just want to see the churches strong; I want to see families strong. We need parents willing to stand up and take their homes back! If we're going to have eyes to see and ears to hear, that doesn't start at the altar in a church; it begins at an altar in your home! We've got to start creating spaces where God can speak and give instructions for the next season.

We need our children to be comfortable in God's presence, not terrified or confused by it. Our homes need Jesus. I ask you, Remnant, to take a stand, create a space, lay your position aside, and get into His presence. Let God speak to you, and be diligent with the Word! Even if that means you must change your plans to align with His, I'm telling you, it's worth it! He is giving you the eyes to see what you've never seen, ears to hear what you've never heard, and the ability to carry out everything He is showing you!

> *"But if serving the Lord seems undesirable to you, then choose for yourselves this day whom you will serve... But as for me and my household, we will serve the Lord."*
> *- Joshua 24:15*

What are you believing God to do in your life this season, and how can you create a space for Him to move in?

_____
_____
_____
_____
_____
_____
_____
_____
_____
_____
_____
_____
_____

DAY 3
CHANGE YOUR POSITION

I could use many people for today's topic, but none better than Zacchaeus. Sometimes, you've got to change your position to get a glimpse of Jesus and stand in His presence. The Bible said Zacchaeus was short and wealthy! His stature and status were not going to determine his next opportunity. He was not too good to climb a tree. Zacchaeus was not afraid to get his hands dirty to see Jesus, and because of this, he got Jesus' attention! We live in a world that refuses to be inconvenienced to get into His presence. We have knees that have never hit the floor, but we expect miracles. People want to hear Him speak but refuse to walk away from the chaos.

Zacchaeus laid his position aside to position himself with Jesus. Once Zacchaeus was in Jesus' presence, conviction hit his heart. So many people live without conviction because they haven't even entered His presence. If you want to have eyes to see and ears to hear, you've got to change the position where you are now. LEAN INTO His presence and prepare for an encounter!

> "A man was there by the name of Zacchaeus; he was a chief tax collector and was wealthy. He wanted to see who Jesus was, but because he was short, he could not see over the crowd. So he ran ahead and climbed a sycamore-fig tree to see him."
> - Luke 19:2-4

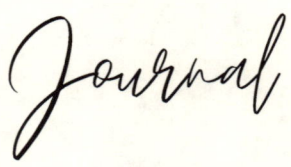

Are you too comfortable where you are? Do you feel God is calling you to change your position to move forward?

_____
_____
_____
_____
_____
_____
_____
_____
_____
_____
_____
_____
_____

DAY 4
CREATE A SPACE

When you commit yourself and your home to the Lord, He will give insight that will cause you to become bold in your decisions. You will begin to walk by faith and not by sight. Many people live a life without faith. Therefore, they can only see what's right in front of them. They will make decisions based on what's reasonable rather than what's possible. Prophetic insight will cause you to take a leap of faith when it doesn't make sense to anyone else because you know it's possible with God.

As you grow in God and He reveals more, you will begin to trust His Word over what you see with your physical eye. You will start seeing the world from His perspective, not your own. You'll understand that cancer is only a word, and sickness can be healed. You'll know that miracles, signs, and wonders are not something we hope for, but we can experience them because God is that good. You've just got to have faith and know what He says. Create a space for God to do something GREAT!

> *"Jesus answered them, "Have faith in God."*
> *- Mark 11:22*

Are you taking leaps of faith as a result of God's insight, or is your faith lacking in this season?

_____
_____
_____
_____
_____
_____
_____
_____
_____
_____
_____
_____
_____
_____

DAY 5
PARTIAL OBEDIENCE

When God gives you insight, it's your obligation to make a move! Remember, partial obedience is still disobedience. If God asks you to do something and only do it halfway, you're walking in disobedience to His Word. Too many people have received a Word and have only fulfilled part of it. Too often, we want God to do His part before we do ours.

When He called the disciples, He said, "Follow me, and I will..." I believe God hasn't "done" because we haven't first followed. He told Abraham to leave His father's house, and then He would make him the father of many nations. If Abraham had never left his father's house, nothing else would have come about. When God gives you insight into your life and the lives of your household, don't give partial obedience! Jump in, and don't hold back.

When you create a space to hear God, He will speak, but then you must move on the Word!

> And he said to them, "Follow me, and
> I will make you fishers of men."
> - Matthew 4:19

What is one move you would make if you knew nothing was holding you back?

DAY 6
DON'T STOP SHORT

God has given you the ability to do great things! Stop letting comparison hold you back from being who God called you, and take responsibility for your life! You could be on the edge of something great; comparison could be trying to talk you out of it! Too many people stop short of what God wants for their lives. We give up right before it's time to take a step! We stop short of the promises given to us by God. Remember, every promise of God spoken over your life is YES and AMEN!

Let me be the one to remind you today not to settle here; this is not the place God has for you. He is inviting you to step into something you've never seen before. As you create a space for God, He will speak and give insight for your NEXT. If you don't recognize what God is doing, you will invest your time and energy in the wrong things and head in the wrong direction. Let the Holy Spirit lead as you step into your future and help you.

> "For all the promises of God in Him are Yes, and in Him Amen, to the glory of God through us."
> **- 2 Corinthians 1:20**

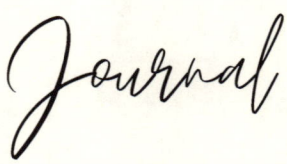

Can you feel the change in the atmosphere
and the pull into something new?

_____
_____
_____
_____
_____
_____
_____
_____
_____
_____
_____
_____
_____

DAY 7
STAY FOCUSED

To reach your NEXT in God, you've got to stay focused on the Word of the Lord! When all else fails, the Word never will. The world does a great job keeping our minds bogged down with negative things! The Bible tells us to keep our minds on the Word and think about things that are true, noble, right, pure, lovely, admirable, excellent, and praiseworthy. As you move with God, you must be selective of what you think about, meditate on, and listen to! If the enemy can distract you with "things," you'll stop taking steps forward! When you're focused on what is right, you'll begin to run and not grow weary!

We are in a crucial time, a decision-making season. Will you continue forward, or will you allow the enemy to cause a halt in your advancement? It's time for the Remannt to take a stand and keep declaring the Word! Today, make a conscious effort to focus! Replace negative thoughts with positive affirmations and reminders of God's goodness, and whatever you do, don't stop moving forward!

> *Finally, brothers and sisters, whatever is true, whatever is noble, whatever is right, whatever is pure, whatever is lovely, whatever is admirable—if anything is excellent or praiseworthy—think about such things."*
> *- Philippians 4:8*

What are the negative things around you that are trying to steal your focus? Make a list. How can you be more mindful against them?

_____
_____
_____
_____
_____
_____
_____
_____
_____
_____
_____
_____
_____

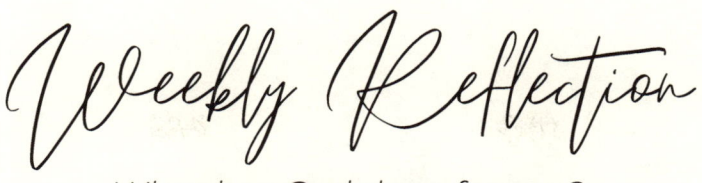

What has God done for you?

_____
_____
_____
_____
_____
_____
_____
_____
_____
_____
_____
_____
_____
_____

Week Two

DAY 8
IN SPIRIT AND IN TRUTH

Worship begins with acknowledging God's greatness and our dependence on Him. I pray that we, the Church, posture our hearts in worship. True worship is marked by humility and surrender. Just as a flock trusts its shepherd, we must entrust our lives to God. As we bow before Him, may we lay aside our worries, doubts, and distractions and allow our hearts to be fully open to His presence.

John says, "Those who worship Him must worship in Spirit and in truth." Worship was never meant to be filled with moments of what we can get from God, but how much more can we give Him? Worship is an intimate moment between you and God. It's where you understand that "though He slays me, yet I will hope and trust in Him." When we return to the heart of worship, we lay our agenda aside to sit at His feet.

"I'm comin' back to the heart of worship
And it's all about You
It's all about You, Jesus"

"God is spirit, and those who worship him must worship in Spirit and in truth."
*- **John 4:24**

What does worship mean to you personally?

_____
_____
_____
_____
_____
_____
_____
_____
_____
_____
_____
_____
_____
_____
_____

DAY 9
ESCAPE VS ENCOUNTER

In the book of Exodus, Moses led the Children of Israel out of Egypt, where the Egyptians had enslaved them for generations. Moses encountered God at a burning bush, where He would get instructions to go before Pharoah. Moses declared, "Let my people go so we can go into the wilderness to worship our God." After the plagues came, the people were released, and the Children of Israel crossed the Red Sea. They were on their way to their Promised Land, but the worship was not in their hearts. They were still angry and hurt, and escaping was their priority, not realizing that God already made a way. Moses had an encounter with God that he desired to lead others to. The people only wanted to be free from their natural burdens. They could not wait for escape, but Moses couldn't wait for the next encounter.

When you worship God, do you worship for an escape from your reality or for the reality of encountering Yahweh? If you only want to escape from something you're going through, you've missed it. Position yourself to encounter God, and your reality will change.

> "The Lord, the God of the Hebrews, has sent me to tell you: Let my people go, so that they may worship me in the wilderness. But so far you have not listened."
> - **Exodus 7:16**

Are you worshipping for escape or encounter?

DAY 10
OBEDIENCE OR SACRIFICE

The people cried out for a king. They wanted to be like all the other nations even though the Lord had led them through the voice of Samuel. Saul from the tribe of Benjamin was chosen and anointed King. He led well for a brief time. He was small in his own eyes, yet God allowed him to become great. Saul, on coronation day, was hiding among the baggage. He was an insecure leader who wanted to ensure the people were pleased, costing him the Kingdom.

Saul had one problem. He worshiped God out of His agenda. In 1 Samuel 15, Saul was instructed to destroy everything of the Amalekites because they had harmed the Israelites as they came up from Egypt. The Amalekites were a true enemy of God, but the people convinced King Saul to keep the good and the strength of the Amalekites, including King Agag. But everything despised and weak they destroyed.

King Saul's excuse? He wanted to worship God and offer sacrifice. But this wasn't the sacrifice God required. Saul was disobedient to the Lord because he feared man over God and wanted to please them over Him. He wanted worship and honor from the people instead of giving God genuine praise and authentic worship! Samuel says these convicting words to the King, "Obedience is better than sacrifice. And rebellion is as the sin of witchcraft."

> "Rebellion is as sinful as witchcraft, and stubbornness as bad as worshiping idols. So because you have rejected the command of the LORD, he has rejected you as king."
> - *1 Samuel 15:23*

Are you being obedient to what God is asking of you? Are you worshipping and honoring Him with obedience or sacrifice?

_____
_____
_____
_____
_____
_____
_____
_____
_____
_____
_____
_____
_____
_____

DAY 11
THROUGH OR TO

TThe Kingdom of Israel was torn from Saul the day he disobeyed God. Saul was grieved because of the loss of position in man's eyes. He cried, "Please don't take the Kingdom from me." A distressing spirit came over Saul, and the only thing that soothed it for a moment was the harp playing of a young shepherd boy who desired to worship God in Spirit and truth. David became the instrument of worship that soothed the disobedience of another.

Worship brings peace into the atmosphere; when you worship the True King, troubles vanish, and hearts are lifted! We were created to worship; therefore, we will fix our eyes on something. Our hearts will be turned to something. May it be turned to Jesus, the son of David—the one who brings peace and destroys every enemy of God in your life. May your life song sing to Him. Regardless of what your worship sounds like, your sound is meant for the hearing of one King on the throne! It poses the question for you today, Remnant:

Will you become the instrument for His song to play through, or will you desire to be played to?

> *"Whenever the spirit from God came on Saul, David would pick up his lyre and play, and Saul would then be relieved, feel better, and the evil spirit would leave him."*
> - 1 Samuel 16:23

Will you become the instrument for His song to play through, or will you desire to be played to?

_____
_____
_____
_____
_____
_____
_____
_____
_____
_____
_____
_____
_____

DAY 12
POSTURE OVER POSITION

Sometimes, we write devotionals, preach sermons, and sing worship songs that lift a heavy spirit or burden from people's hearts. But Jesus didn't come for a temporary fix; He came to destroy the works of darkness.

David had an encounter with God through the prophet Samuel. Samuel heard the word of the Lord to go to Jesse's house, David's father. David had seven older, handsome brothers who looked like they could be the next King of Israel. But they were not who God chose. God was looking for the diligent one who was tending to the sheep. The one who would nurture, cover, and anoint the wounds of those in the field. The one who would destroy the bear and lion that would come in with the desire to harm the little lambs. The one who would sing worship to God in the open air while no one was watching. David's life was an instrument for God's glory.

David never thought about being his father's first pick. He never refused the anointing, although he was last in line. He accepted what God brought before him. It was never about David's status; it was always about His heart. God is looking for a people not concerned with a title but with posture. David postured himself before the Lord, and even in times of mistakes, he was quick to repent. When you posture yourself right, you will experience God's glory and walk with an anointing.

> "Then the Lord said, "Anoint him, for he is the one."
> - *1 Samuel 16:12*

Have you been concerned with the title more than posture? What does your posture look like today?

_____
_____
_____
_____
_____
_____
_____
_____
_____
_____
_____
_____
_____
_____

DAY 13
LIVE IN ENCOUNTER

David was anointed by the prophet Samuel to be King of Israel. He had an encounter even though it took years and many life-threatening situations to come to pass. The encounter came to Him, but David would have to learn to live IN encounter to survive. Because of David's close encounters with God, he wrote things like Psalm 23, "Though I walk through the valley of the shadow of death, I will fear no evil, for you are with me!" His worship was never contingent on how he felt or His situation. David knew that God was, He is, and He always will be. Even when David sinned, his cry wasn't "Don't take this position from me!"; instead, it was a true reflection of His heart. David would cry, "Lord, don't take your PRESENCE from me!"

David knew from personal experience what he wrote in Psalms 16:11, "In His presence is the fullness of Joy, and At His right hand, there are pleasures forever more." The story goes down in history that of David's Kingdom, there would be no end.

You will long to stay in His presence when you worship God with a pure heart. And even in the most vulnerable times, you will find refuge in the Lord. Having a title means nothing without God's presence. We've got to learn how to LIVE IN ENCOUNTER, not just have them occasionally.

> "In His presence is the fullness of Joy, and At His right hand, there are pleasures forever more."
> **- 1 Psalms 16:11**

When in your life have you felt something slipping away from you? What was your response?

_____
_____
_____
_____
_____
_____
_____
_____
_____
_____
_____
_____
_____
_____

DAY 14
DON'T GET DISTRACTED

The enemy does not have to defeat you; he only needs to distract you. If he can distract you, he stunts your growth and keeps you from moving forward. All distractions are not bad sometimes; they keep us too busy. Martha was not doing something terrible, but she was distracted when Jesus entered the room. She was preparing for an encounter she was too busy to participate in. The preparations must be made, but not at the expense of the encounter!

We've got to learn how to lay some things down in the season of movement. We can't carry everything! Our hands cannot get so full that we cannot run with what God has placed in them. We must position our hearts in worship so we never miss a moment. Don't get distracted and begin sinking in the water around you, Peter. Your purpose is too great, and your movement is mighty! God has called you for such a time as this!

> "let your eyes look directly forward, and your gaze straight ahead."
> - **Proverbs 4:25**

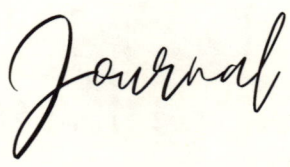

Have you felt distracted lately? What has the enemy been distracting you from?

_____
_____
_____
_____
_____
_____
_____
_____
_____
_____
_____
_____
_____
_____

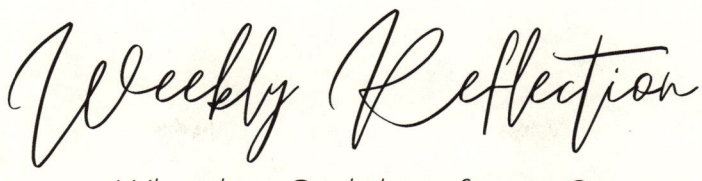

What has God done for you?

_____
_____
_____
_____
_____
_____
_____
_____
_____
_____
_____
_____
_____
_____
_____

Week Three

DAY 15
DECLARE THE WORD

Pastor Darlene Bishop, a great friend, once said, "Your Life Follows Your Words." She has been through some trying times, but she is an excellent example that your life is a reflection of the Words you speak. Jesus tells us in Mark 11 that whatever you say and believe in your heart will be done. Even when you don't see what you're believing for, you've got to keep believing until you see it come to pass!

If you believe in healing, KEEP SPEAKING IT and walk in it! How? You walk in faith by living like it's already here. Stop speaking defeat and sickness over your life, but start declaring healing and wholeness! Each morning, your feet hit the floor, and you begin to express the Word over your day, even if your life is contrary to it! You may feel sick, but instead of talking about it, say, "I AM HEALTHY," "I AM MADE WHOLE," or "I AM HEALED."

Declare the Word over your life, believe the Word, and watch God change some things. As Pastor Darlene would say, "Watch your mouth and let God be God."

> "Truly, I say to you, whoever says to this mountain, 'Be taken up and thrown into the sea,' and does not doubt in his heart, but believes that what he says will come to pass, it will be done for him."
> - Mark 11:23

Write down a few declarations with scripture and declare them over your life this week!

DAY 16
MORE THAN A CONQUEROR

When defeat looks you in the face, remember that God has already given you victory. The Bible says you are MORE than a conqueror through Jesus. Don't let the enemy cause you to return to a season you have outgrown! When the enemy starts throwing old things at you, you've got to remember what God has said about you! Get ahold of the Word of God and speak it over your life. Keep the vision in front of you. God said you are a conqueror regardless of what is thrown at you!

There is often a season of waiting before you see the promise come to pass! The enemy likes to play with your mind during those times to cause doubt to rise in your life. You've got to stand on the Word and surround yourself with people who believe the Word with you. Good, Godly friends are essential in this walk! They will encourage you on the dark days and celebrate with you on the glory days! The enemy picks us apart when we are isolated, but messing with a group of anointed, Holy Ghost-filled believers is a little more challenging!

> "In all these things we are more than conquerors through him who loved us."
> - **Roman 8:37**

Has the enemy tried throwing old issues at you? What was your response?

DAY 17
KEEP DECLARING

In the beginning, God created everything by speaking it into existence! He taught us from the start that our words hold power! The Bible says in Job 22:29, "You will declare a thing, and it will be established for you!" You must manage every word that comes from your mouth. Every word has the opportunity to build up or tear down. If what you're speaking isn't profiting your life, CHANGE YOUR WORDS! We cannot keep moving forward in God if our words contradict His!

I encourage you to wake up every day and begin speaking His Word, and you'll create a world filled with His goodness. Begin to declare life, health, and peace over your family, and let God be God! If your world contradicts His Word, keep speaking it until you see it come to pass! Believe when you deliver a thing, it will be established! Faith is the evidence of things yet to be seen! You must have faith in your heart and confess it with your mouth! Don't lose faith, but keep declaring His Word!

"You will also declare a thing, And it will be established for you..."
- Job 22:29

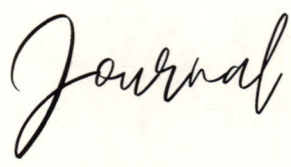

Have your words been building up or tearing down your life this last season? What world have you created with your words?

_____
_____
_____
_____
_____
_____
_____
_____
_____
_____
_____
_____
_____
_____

DAY 18
CONSISTENCY IS KEY

People don't stumble upon destiny; they plan and take steps toward it. If you're waiting for your dream to hit you like a ton of bricks one random day, you're mistaken! You've got to make a plan, pray, declare, and take steps toward it. Destiny doesn't come in one big step; it comes by taking small steps over time. Consistency is KEY! This is the season we will plan, pray, declare, and step! What are you expecting God to do as we begin this new year and season? What dream has He given you? What promise has He given your family?

In Colossians 3:2, Paul tells us to focus more on God's goals than on our own, to fix our minds on things above. Having dreams is great, but do they line up with the Word? Taking your next steps means setting goals that get you closer to Jesus daily. So, as you plan, ensure it aligns with God's will for your life and draws you closer to Him. And when they begin to come to pass, don't forget God.

> "Set your minds on things that are above, not on things that are on earth."
> - **Colossians 3:2**

Journal

What is one thing God has spoken to you for THIS season? What scripture backs this Word? Write it down.

_____

_____

_____

_____

_____

_____

_____

_____

_____

_____

_____

_____

DAY 19
YOU'VE BEEN TESTED

We are in a season where holding onto the promises of God is critical! If you're not intentional about your walk with God, the enemy can easily throw you off course. Jesus says in John 10:10, the thief comes to steal, kill, and destroy what God has given you! We have a purpose in this life; we carry an anointing, and the enemy is trying to distract us. If he cannot steal it from you, he will distract you and try to get you to lay it down.

Stay focused! Many of you reading this are coming off a "wilderness season." You have felt lost, confused, and unsure of your call, but you've been declaring the Word!! You've been tested, tried, and thrown into the fire, but you're coming out not even smelling like smoke! You're not even looking like what we've been through!

Spend a few moments today and pray about this week. Ask God to reveal any traps the enemy has set before you. Ask Him to give you the strength and wisdom to continue!

> *"The thief comes only to steal and kill and destroy; I have come that they may have life, and have it to the full."*
> *- John 10:10*

Write down any specific prayers and anything God speaks to you during your devotion today.

_____
_____
_____
_____
_____
_____
_____
_____
_____
_____
_____
_____
_____

DAY 20
ALL THINGS ARE POSSIBLE

Today, I want you to speak, declare, and stand on God's promises for your life! It is one thing to hear the Word, but another when you open your mouth and believe it! What God brings to your life can only come in His power, not yours. When God places a dream, vision, or ministry in your heart, it should be unattainable in your strength! God does this, so we rely on Him; only He can take the credit!

Always take God at His Word! We trust Him to grow our faith and allow us to accomplish all He says is possible. It will always be impossible with man, but with Jesus, ALL THINGS ARE POSSIBLE! Don't give up before you see the promise, even when life seems to be working against you. You're exactly where you need to be! Stand on His Word and know it will come to pass!

> *"Jesus looked at them and said, 'With man this is impossible, but with God all things are possible."*
> *- Matthew 19:26*

Journal

What's one situation you're facing that seems impossible?

_____
_____
_____
_____
_____
_____
_____
_____
_____
_____
_____
_____
_____

DAY 21
DREAM AGAIN

I'm the kind of person that is always up for adventure! In Spring 2022, my sister-in-law, Krystal, and I decided to board a plane and go to Africa with little time to plan. Nothing will stop me from taking the step when I feel God's calling! When our church began looking for a new building, and we walked onto the campus at Cross Plains, I knew that was it. Aaron and I didn't have the money to purchase that building, BUT GOD DID. We didn't have the means to move our entire congregation to a new location, BUT GOD DID! We trusted Him through the unknown!

Jeremiah 33:3 says God will "tell you things you don't know and can't figure out." Are you there today? Are you stuck in a place wanting to experience something new but can't quite figure out how it will happen? It's okay; God can show you, but you've got to trust that His plan is better than your own! God has so many wonders to experience; we must follow His lead! Some of you have laid down the adventure you were supposed to experience. You settled for something lesser, but God is here today telling you to pick up the dream again, go after the desire, and participate in the wonder.

> "Ask me, and I will tell you things that you don't know and can't find out."
> - Jeremiah 33:3

Do you really trust God with the "unknown?" What adventure do you feel God is calling you to?

_____
_____
_____
_____
_____
_____
_____
_____
_____
_____
_____
_____
_____
_____
_____

Weekly Reflection

What has God done for you?

_____
_____
_____
_____
_____
_____
_____
_____
_____
_____
_____
_____
_____
_____

Week Four

DAY 22
THE RAIN IS HERE

If you have felt like this season has been one of lack and drought, I believe the rain is coming! Let me prophesy over your life today and say THE RAIN IS HERE! The promise of showers of blessing is one that we find in Ezekiel 34:26, where God speaks to His people through the prophet Ezekiel. In these verses, God promises to bless His people with rain in its season so that the earth may yield its produce and the trees of the field may bear their fruit. This is a powerful promise of provision from God, who is faithful to keep His promises.

As we reflect on this promise, we can see this is not just a promise of physical provision and spiritual renewal. The rain God promises symbolizes His Spirit, which refreshes and restores the dry and weary soul. Just as the earth needs rain to yield its produce, we need the Holy Spirit to bear fruit. The promise of showers of blessing reminds us that God is faithful to provide for our physical and spiritual needs if we trust Him.

> "I will make them and the places surrounding my hill a blessing. I will send down showers in season; there will be showers of blessing."
> - **Ezekiel 34:26**

Journal

What area of your life do you need God's showers of blessings to fall on?

_____
_____
_____
_____
_____
_____
_____
_____
_____
_____
_____
_____
_____
_____
_____

DAY 23
HARVEST IS YIELDING

When discussing harvest time, we think of pumpkin spice and everything nice. It's a season that comes and goes, but I'm talking about living in the perpetual harvest of the Lord! Living in the seed, time, and harvest and continually seeing the harvest coming forth. The harvest of the Lord isn't a season; it's a lifestyle. The rain is falling, and the harvest is yielding! Whatever you've been sowing for is coming to pass! We understand just in the natural; the spiritual seed represents the Word of God, which we receive and plant in our hearts. The rain that God sends represents His Spirit, which brings growth and fruitfulness to our lives. When we sow the Word of God in our hearts and seek to obey His will, He will bring the growth and increase we need to flourish.

Just as the rain nourishes the land and causes the seeds to sprout and grow, God's Spirit nourishes our souls and causes the Word of God to take root and grow in our lives. This promise reminds us that our growth and success depend on God's grace and provision. The rain is coming, and the harvest is springing up; are you ready to receive it? Have you made room to contain the blessing God is pouring out?

> "Then he will send rain for the seed you sow in the ground, and the food that comes from the land will be rich and plentiful..."
> - Isaiah 30:23

Do you believe in your heart that growth and increase is on the way? If not, what's stopping you from believing the Word?

_____
_____
_____
_____
_____
_____
_____
_____
_____
_____
_____
_____
_____
_____

DAY 24
DRY AND BARREN SEASON

In the book of Zechariah, the Lord speaks through the prophet to encourage His people to trust in Him for provision, even in the midst of a dry and barren season. Zechariah 10:1 says, "It is the Lord who sends the thunderstorms. He gives showers of rain to all people and plants of the field to everyone." God is the one who controls the rain and provides for His people. In a dry and barren season, losing hope and giving up on our dreams and goals can be easy. But God encourages us to ask Him for rain, to declare His provision in the midst of the dryness. Just as God gave rain to the Israelites in the wilderness, He promises to provide for us in our times of need.

We are declaring the rain and putting our trust in God! All we can do is be faithful to plant, and it's up to Him to send the rain! God is faithful to His Word and will provide for us according to the riches of His glory. The season cannot dictate your declaration! You must learn how to declare for rain in the storm and the drought!

> *"Ask the Lord for rain in the springtime; it is the Lord who sends the thunderstorms. He gives showers of rain to all people, and plants of the field to everyone."*
> **- Zechariah 10:1 (NIV)**

Is your season dictating your declaration, or are you declaring in spite of what's happening around you?

_____
_____
_____
_____
_____
_____
_____
_____
_____
_____
_____
_____
_____

DAY 25
NO TANGIBLE EVIDENCE

Seasons of preparation will always require faith and perseverance. A great story in 1 Kings tells us that Elijah had been praying for rain for a long time, and at this moment, he heard the sound of rain even though there was no visible sign yet. Elijah believed that God would answer his prayers and send the requested rain.

Like Elijah, we must believe God will answer our prayers, even when we can't see tangible evidence. We may feel our prayers are going unanswered, but we must remember that God always works behind the scenes, even when we can't see it. Elijah didn't give up when he didn't see immediate results from his prayers. Instead, he continued to pray and believed that God would answer his prayers in His perfect timing.

I say all that to tell you, get your seed in the ground! The rain is coming, and for some of you, the rain is here! Every Word and blessing that has been planted is going to spout! You're going to stand in the harvest you've prayed for! BELIEVE IT!

> "And Elijah said to Ahab, "Go, eat and drink, for there is the sound of a heavy rain." So Ahab went off to eat and drink, but Elijah climbed to the top of Carmel, bent down to the ground and put his face between his knees."
> - 1 Kings 18:41-42

What have you put in the ground? What harvest are you EXPECTING to come? Can you hear the SOUND OF RAIN?

_____
_____
_____
_____
_____
_____
_____
_____
_____
_____
_____
_____
_____

DAY 26
TEND THE RIGHT THINGS

In a literal sense, farmers understand the importance of tending to their crops. They must plant the seeds, water them, and care for them until they are ready to be harvested. They will only yield a bountiful harvest with this hard work and dedication. Similarly, in our own lives, we must tend to what we have planted. Whether it is our relationships, careers, personal growth, the Word of the Lord, or finances, we must put in the effort and care to see them flourish. You will end up empty and unfulfilled when you chase unrealistic goals and get lost in things other than God's purpose. BE SURE TO TEND THE RIGHT THINGS with the right people!

We must focus on what truly matters and tend to them carefully and diligently. The Church has to return to a place of consistently pursuing God, not occasionally! We must plant the seeds of faith, nurture them through prayer and study of the Bible, and live out our beliefs in our daily lives. By doing this, we will reap the abundant blessings that come with a life devoted to God. Remember, WHAT YOU PLANT, YOU WILL REAP!! The rain is coming; what are you spending time tending to?

> *"Those who work their land will have abundant food, but those who chase fantasies will have their fill of poverty."*
> *- Proverbs 28:19*

What are you spending time tending to?
What has your attention? If you were to
gather a harvest today, what would you reap?

DAY 27
LOOK ONE MORE TIME

Sometimes, God is just looking for our persistence! Elijah had been praying for rain and believed that God would answer his prayers. Elijah knew it was coming; he knew God would come through like He had many times before. He asked his servant to go up the mountain and look for ANY SIGN that the rain was approaching. After the seventh time, his servant reported to him a small cloud rising from the sea. He knew this cloud was a sign of the rain he had been praying for. It wasn't as big as he thought it would be, but it was enough for God to do something great! Elijah had faith that God would keep His promise to him, and God did.

Let me prophesy over your life today; YOU'RE GOING TO SEE WHAT YOU'VE BEEN BELIEVING FOR! Even though all hope has been lost and there has been no physical sign that it will come, I urge you to LOOK ONE MORE TIME! PRAY ONE MORE TIME! This is not your season to quit; it's your season to LOOK AGAIN!

> "The seventh time the servant reported, 'A cloud as small as a man's hand is rising from the sea.' So Elijah said, 'Go and tell Ahab, "Hitch up your chariot and go down before the rain stops you."'
> **- 1 Kings 18:44**

What is equivalent to "a cloud as small as a man's hand" in your life? What are you looking for that may be already visible but small?

_____
_____
_____
_____
_____
_____
_____
_____
_____
_____
_____
_____
_____

DAY 28
HURRY, THE RAIN WILL STOP YOU

Preparing for rain begins with cultivating faith in God's promises. In 1 Kings, Elijah told the servant to tell King Ahab that the rain was coming and then said, "If you don't hurry, the rain will stop you!" If you don't prepare for what you've been believing for, the blessing may overwhelm you! The rain is coming, the harvest is ready, but ARE YOU? Is your heart ready to receive whom God wants to bring? Is your bank account prepared to invest in the business idea God put in your spirit? You see, it's not just about speaking words; it's about aligning your life with His Word!

Today, as we prepare for the rain, reflect on your faith. Are you confidently trusting that God can still do the immeasurable? Don't just believe in surface-level miracles; believe in the OVERFLOW! Believe what's coming is the greatest harvest and blessing you've ever seen! Now that you believe, it's time to PREPARE! The rain is coming, and if you don't hurry, it WILL stop you!

> "...Then Elijah shouted, "Hurry to Ahab and tell him, 'Climb into your chariot and go back home. If you don't hurry, the rain will stop you!'"
> - 1 Kings 18:44

What situation are you confidently believing God to step in and completely change?

What has God done for you?

_____
_____
_____
_____
_____
_____
_____
_____
_____
_____
_____
_____
_____

Week Five

DAY 29
BE A FRIEND

As this devotion is coming to an end, we know that life is hard, but friends make it better! One of my main goals when encouraging someone is to put good, God-fearing people in their circle. We all need to create a community where you have friends, prayer partners, and encouragers in your corner! Those people are not always easy to find! I encourage you to pray about the people around you, the ones you run to in moments of weakness.

Ecclesiastes 4:9-10 tells us that "two are better than one...for if they fall, one will lift his (her) fellow." So many people sit in churches week after week without a friend to talk to. I challenge you to be a friend, get someone's name and number, pray for them, call them, and encourage them. It's not enough that we do our devotions, go to church, and sing songs; we've got to be a light in this dark world.

You will be surprised at what God will do through you if you open yourself up a little more. Be approachable, kind, and discerning! Nothing is greater than a group of people going after God's heart together!

> "Two are better than one, because they have a good reward for their toil. For if they fall, one will lift up his fellow. But woe to him who is alone when he falls and has not another to lift him up!"
> - *Ecclesiastes 4:9-10*

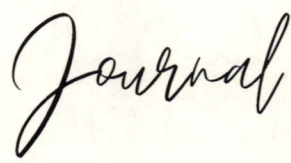

Are you willing to trust God to lead you to a new friend or two?

DAY 30
MOVE FORWARD

Let me speak prophetically over you today! You are moving from this place and will enter your next! The Promise is too great to sit and wait, but NOW is the time to GET UP and ACCOMPLISH the Word God has given you! The movement process can trigger a wave of fear, but we are not a people with a spirit of fear but of POWER, LOVE, and a SOUND MIND. As you move into your NEXT, go in BOLDNESS and declare the Word of God!

Let me give you a warning as well. As you prepare for an encounter, know that you may also encounter what feels like opposition, but don't let it stop you! Moving forward will always sound an alarm to the enemy that you're coming to take territory because God is always leading you to GREATER!

I pray God's peace will surround you, replacing all anxiety with a calm assurance. You will never experience a trouble-free season, but you have a God who has your back when trouble shows its face. Don't let chaos cause you to miss the Promise you've been given! THIS IS YOUR SEASON, LEAN IN HIM and MOVE FORWARD!

> *"For God did not give us the spirit of fear; but of power, and of love, and of a sound mind."*
> *- 2 Timothy 1:7*

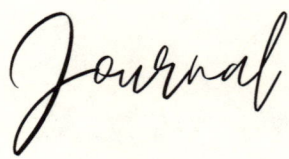

What situation are you confidently believing God to step in and completely change?

_____
_____
_____
_____
_____
_____
_____
_____
_____
_____
_____
_____
_____
_____

Notes

About the Author

Amanda Crabb, along with her husband, Aaron, are the founders and Senior Pastors of Restoring Hope Church in Cross Plains, Tennessee. They have been married since 2001 and have four children; Elijah, Eva, Ean, and Eda-Beth.

Aaron and Amanda Crabb are no strangers to ministry. Having roots in gospel music that has crossed genres, generational boundaries, as well as denominational barriers, they understand the power of His presence in a room filled with thousands as well as the privacy of their own home. Their true passion is preaching the word of God and empowering people to live out their full potential in Christ Jesus. They take the mandate of "Restoring Hope" and release it everywhere they go. Seeing the sick healed, marriages mended, and even seeing the dead raised, they believe that nothing shall be impossible for those who believe.

Pastor Amanda is a mentor to Remnant and a spiritual mother to many. Aaron and Amanda are the Founders of Hope Academy and the first-time Authors of NEXT. Pastor Amanda is honored to be a featured conference speaker who is known for her distinctive message and obedience to the Holy Spirit.

Made in the USA
Columbia, SC
30 September 2023